PRIVATE EYE

BUMPER
BOOK OF COVERS

Published by Private Eye Productions Limited
6 Carlisle Street, London W1
in association with André Deutsch Limited
105 Great Russell Street, London WC1

© Pressdram Limited.

ISBN 233 97699 X

Printed in Great Britain by Kingsdale Press, Reading

The First Bubble Cover.

PRIVATE EYE

incorporating THE FLESH'S WEEKLY

VOL I No 4   Wednesday 7th February 1962   Price 6d.

BRITAIN'S
FIRST
MAN
INTO
SPACE

ALBERT GRISTLE
AWAITS
BLAST-OFF

ho ho very satirical

Britain and U.S. continue with
nuclear tests.

PRIVATE EYE

A FORTNIGHTLY LAMPOON

Vol. 1 No. 9   Thursday 19th. April 1962   Price 1/-

TESTING THE WORLD AWAY

Early attack on George Brown.

PRIVATE EYE

A FORTNIGHTLY LAMPOON

Vol. 1 No. 10   Friday 4th. May 1962   Price 1/-

The poet Milligan speaks — page 9

Official opening of Coventry cathedral.

PRIVATE EYE

No. 12
Friday
1 June 62

Price 1/-

COVENTRY OPENED

Selwyn Lloyd, Chancellor of the Exchequer, dismissed in Macmillan purge.

PRIVATE EYE

No. 16
riday
7 July 62

Price 1/-

De Gaulle vetoes Britain's bid to join the Common Market.

PRIVATE EYE

No. 29
Friday
25 January 63

Price 1/-

Minister of Defence John Profumo
talks to Geoffrey Rippon.

PRIVATE EYE

No. 34
Friday
April 63

Price 1/-

Mandy Rice-Davis, star of the Profumo affair.

PRIVATE EYE

No. 42
Friday
26 July 63

Price 1/-

Publication of the Denning Report
on the Profumo affair.

PRIVATE EYE

No 46
Friday
20 Sept. 63

Price 1/-

Gerald Scarfe.

DENNING IS SERVED

Macmillan resigns. 'Old colleague' is R. A. Butler.

PRIVATE EYE

No 49
Friday
1 Nov. 63

Price 1/-

In the autumn tranquillity of his days while the golden leaves fall silently to the ground an old man, his faithful wife by his side, sits peacefully in the park happy in the knowledge of a lifetime's work well done, a country served and an old colleague stabbed ruthlessly in the back...

John Bloom the washing machine
King in trouble over package
holiday scheme.

PRIVATE EYE

No 65
Friday
12 June 64

1/-

This is the last time I go on a John Bloom Holiday

Right wing Senator Goldwater
was Republican Candidate in
Presidential Elections.

PRIVATE EYE

No 67
Friday
10 July 64

1/-

WORLD PEACE | GOLDWATER SPEAKS

The Queen reads speech for
Wilson's first Labour government.

PRIVATE EYE

No 75
Friday
30 October 64

1/6

QUEEN OPENS PARLIAMENT

HOW MANY POOVES ARE THERE IN WILSON'S GOVERNMENT?   see page 3.

Wilson publicity stresses humble home life.

PRIVATE EYE

N.S.M.A.P.M.A.F.C.K.U.P. (SEE P. 13)

No 77
Friday
27 November 64

1/6

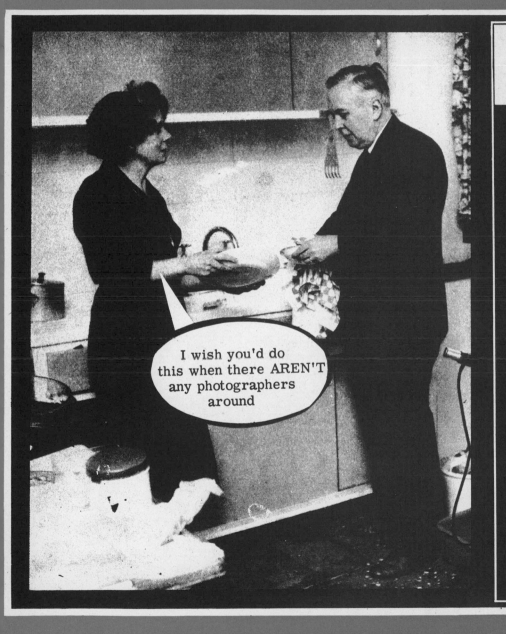

I wish you'd do this when there AREN'T any photographers around

HAROLD DRIES UP AT LAST

MRS. WILSON'S DIARY

SEE PAGE 14

Wilson gives uncritical support
to U.S. Vietnamese policy.

PRIVATE EYE

o. 88
riday
0 April 65

1/6

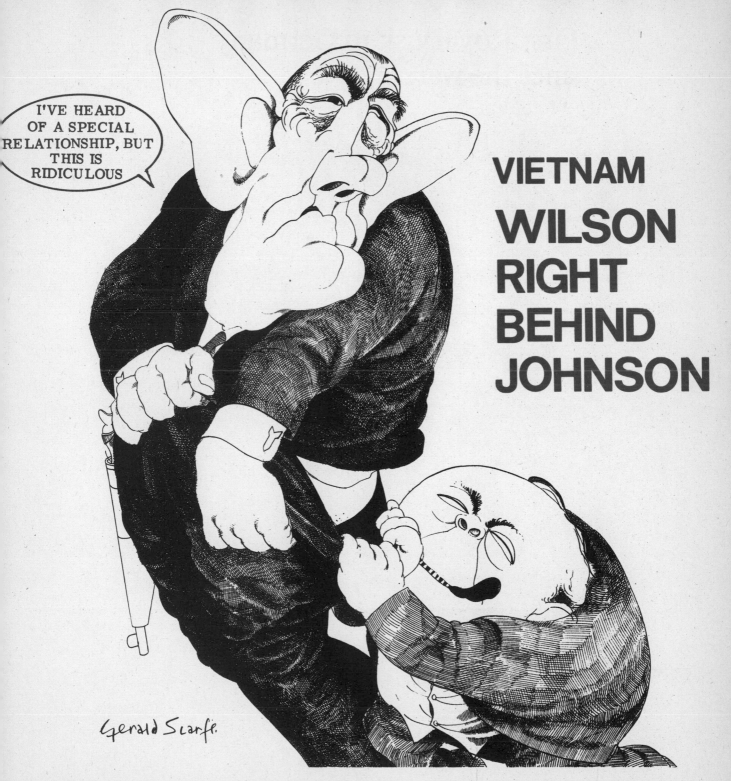

I'VE HEARD OF A SPECIAL RELATIONSHIP, BUT THIS IS RIDICULOUS

VIETNAM

WILSON

RIGHT

BEHIND

JOHNSON

Gerald Scarfe.

First Royal visit to Germany
since the war.

PRIVATE EYE

No. 90
Friday
28 May 65

1/6

SPECIAL ISSUE **ANGLO GERMAN RELATIONS**

IS BEAVERBROOK STILL ALIVE ?

SEE PAGE 14

Edward Heath goes on holiday.

PRIVATE EYE

No. 99
Friday
1 Oct. 65

1/6

Wilson develops close ties with Royalty.

PRIVATE EYE

No. 102
Friday
12 Nov. 65

1/6

First visit by Archbishop of Canterbury
to the Vatican since the Reformation.

No. 112
Friday,
1 April '66.

PRIVATE EYE

1/6

Early photograph of the moon's surface.

PRIVATE EYE

No. 117
Friday,
June 66

1/6

PRIVATE EYE

The Pound under pressure yet again.

PRIVATE EYE

o. 120
riday
July 66

1/6

YOURS FOR 5/-

(in three months time)

Disillusionment with Labour
Government following Wilson's
'July measures'.

PRIVATE EYE

No. 121
Friday
Aug 66

1/6

Brothers, we're on our way out

Assassination of S. African
premier Dr Verwoerd.

PRIVATE EYE

No. 124
Friday
7 Sept. 66

1/6

VERWOERD

A NATION MOURNS

Wilson and Brown investigate
the Common Market.

PRIVATE EYE

No. 134
iday
Feb. 67

1/6

Le seul Journal satirique du Monde

Wilson calls for a 'Great Debate'
on the Common Market.

PRIVATE EYE

No. 141.
Friday
12 May 67

1/6

COMMON MARKET

THE GREAT
DEBATE BEGINS

Coloured cricketer Basil D'Oliveira
(right) refused admission to
S. Africa.

PRIVATE EYE

o. 176
riday
3 Sept. '68

1/6

GOODBYE DOLLY !

We must leave you out

Beatle John Lennon on drugs charge.

PRIVATE EYE

No. 179
Friday
25 Oct. '68

1/6

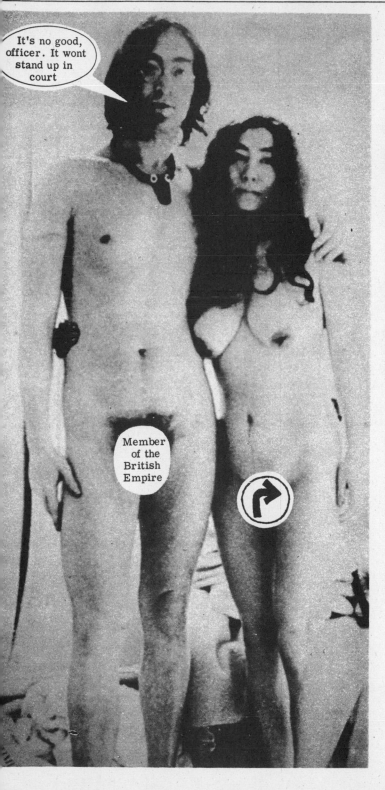

BEATLE HELD

SENSATION

★

SPECIAL REVOLTING ISSUE

All human filth is here

(including Robert Maxwell)

Jackie Kennedy marries
Aristotle Onassis.

PRIVATE EYE

No. 180
Friday
8 Nov. '68

1/6

Richard Nixon becomes U.S. President.
Spiro Agnew is Vice-President.

No. 181
Friday
22 Nov. '68

PRIVATE EYE

NIXON IN BY CLOSE SHAVE!!

1/6

Enoch Powell launches crusade against coloured immigrants.

PRIVATE EYE

No. 182
Friday
6 Dec. '68

1/6

and I tell you some of them have got them this long!

POWELL NEW OUTBURST

Private Eye Editor (left) receives award.

PRIVATE EYE

o. 185
riday
7 Jan. '69

1/6

WINNER OF *GRANADA TV* 'IRRITANT OF THE YEAR' AWARD

Ian Paisley (centre) emerges as leader of hard line Ulster protestants.

PRIVATE EYE

No. 186
Friday
31 Jan. '69

1/6

UP FOR THE CUP

Christians United 4 Belfast Hooligans 0

Ronnie and Reggie Kray
sentenced to life imprisonment.

PRIVATE EYE

No. 189
Friday
14 March
'69 2/-

Those were the Krays...

Are you appealing?

You'd better ask my friends in high places, ducky.

Which twin has the Toni? **Picture by DAVID OLD BAILEY**

Callaghan makes abortive anti–
Wilson coup.

PRIVATE EYE

o. 191
riday
1 April 69

2/-

Euthanasia controversy.

PRIVATE EYE

No. 193
Friday
9 May 69

2/-

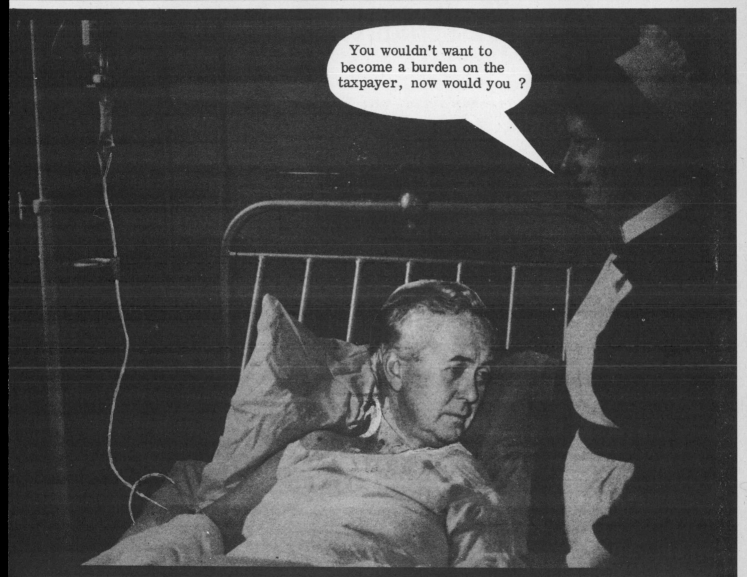

Chauvinist crudity.

PRIVATE EYE

o. 194
riday
3 May '69

WHITSUN MUST GO

Oh What lovely oars !

AXEMAN WAS HEART DONOR — SHOCK

The Queen is acclaimed for her performance in a television documentary.

PRIVATE EYE

No. 197
Friday
4 July 69

2/-

It's the BBC, they want us to do a series

QUEEN TOPS TV POPS

Ulster's Bernadette Devlin visits
America.

PRIVATE EYE

No. 202
Friday
12 Sept. 69

2/-

General Election 1970, won by Heath.

PRIVATE EYE

No. 220
Friday
22 May '70

I never thought he could pull it off three times running

2/-

You've never had it so good

and I've never had it!

THEY'RE OFF!

(OR NOT - as this issue went to press before any announcement was made)

Rumours of disharmony at
Kensington Palace.

PRIVATE EYE

No. 226
Friday
14 Aug. '70.

2/-

TONY & MARGARET —The Truth

Mick Jagger weds Bianca in France.

PRIVATE EYE

No. 246
Friday
May '71
10p

THAT WEDDING

SOUVENIR ISSUE

Visit to Britain of Japanese Emperor.

PRIVATE EYE

No. 256
Friday
8 Oct. '71

10p

Ah so's to you, too matey!

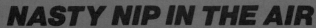

NASTY NIP IN THE AIR

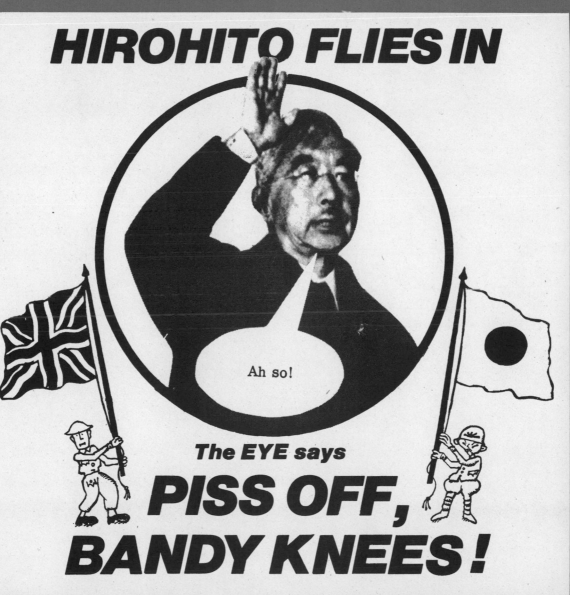

HIROHITO FLIES IN

Ah so!

The EYE says

PISS OFF, BANDY KNEES!

Thalidomide parents sue
Distillers Co.

PRIVATE EYE

No. 285
Friday
17 Nov. '72

10p

THALIDOMIDE CASE

They haven't got a leg to stand on

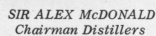

SIR ALEX McDONALD
Chairman Distillers

Chairman's Statement

Cyril Smith (left) elected for Rochdale.

PRIVATE EYE

No. 287
Friday
Dec. '72

10p

LIBERAL REVIVAL

The Watergate Scandal.

PRIVATE EYE

No. 297
Friday
4 May '73

12p

Vice-President Spiro Agnew resigns.

PRIVATE EYE

No. 309
Friday
19 Oct. '73

12p

Agnew and Nixon

The Last Fare~well

Goodbye Sir

AAARGH!

Marcia Williams given life peerage.

PRIVATE EYE

No. 325
Friday
May '74

12p

IT'S LADY SLAGHEAP!

WILSON'S SHOCKER

I.R.A. funeral procession in Kilburn.

PRIVATE IRA

o. 326
riday
June '74

12p

SPONSORED WALK
HELP THE BLIND

Edward Heath loses election
and comes under fire.

PRIVATE EYE

No. 335
Friday
Oct. '74

12p

TORIES CONSIDER HEATH'S FUTURE

Arab influence grows.

PRIVATE EYE

No. 340
...day
...Jan.'75

12p

BRITAIN SOLD SHOCK

My wives and I . . .

New Man at Palace

President Amin makes joke.

PRIVATE EYE

.353
day
June '75

15p

Runaway M.P. John Stonehouse
brought back to Britain.

PRIVATE EYE

o. 355
riday
th July '75

15p

STONEHOUSE FLIES IN

North Sea Oil begins to flow.

PRIVATE EYE

No. 363
Friday
14 Nov. '75

15p

Now British Oil.

Inaugural flight of Concorde.

PRIVATE EYE

No. 368
Friday
Jan. '76

15p

UP AND AWAY!

Will the passenger please fasten his safety belt

It's the Bahrain Drain !

Reports of Princess Margaret's
romance with playboy
Roddy Llewellyn.

PRIVATE EYE

371
day
March '76

15p

Read all about it, ma'am! "Princess Margaret and the Playboy — Amazing Shock Horror"

We are not amazed

QUEEN IN FLEET ST.

EXCLUSIVE PICTURE

Harold Wilson resigns.

No.373
Friday
April '76

PRIVATE EYE

15p

END OF AN ERA

Jeremy Thorpe, liberal leader, resigns.

PRIVATE EYE

376
ay
lay '76
15p

THORPE RESIGNS SHOCK

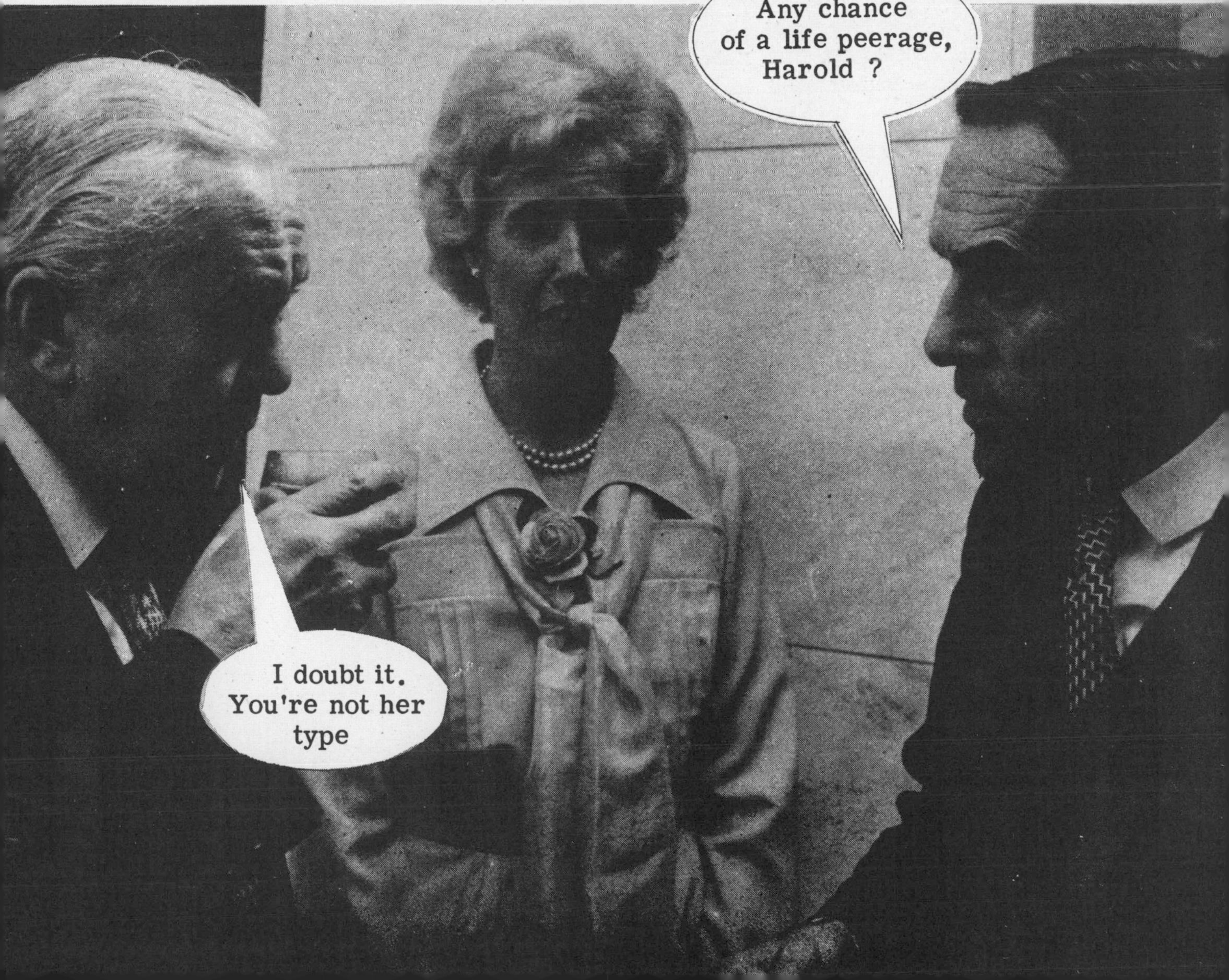

President Ford makes fatal gaffe.

PRIVATE EYE

387
day
Oct.'76

20p

Wilson and Maudling both beneficiaries
of crooked property man Sir Eric Miller
who committed suicide.

President Sadat makes historic trip to Israel.

PRIVATE EYE

No.416
Friday
Nov.'77

25p

WIND OF CHANGE IN MIDDLE EAST

I hope there isn't going to be a split

Shift in Tory policy on immigration.

PRIVATE EYE

422
day
Feb.'78

25p

New Tory Blue
forces Black out

Jeremy Thorpe comes under fire.

PRIVATE EYE

435

uy

ug. 78

25p

Gannex-King Lord Kagan on the run.

PRIVATE EYE

444

ec. '78

25p

Service of
LESSONS &
CAROLS

And lo!
Kagan went unto
Israel for he was
sore afraid of
the Fuzz

Jim Callaghan calls a General Election.

PRIVATE EYE

No. 453
Friday.
April '79.

25p

Mrs Thatcher wins the Election for the Conservatives.

PRIVATE EYE

. 454
day
May '79

25p

Wake up!
It's a New Dawn
for Britain!

Jeremy Thorpe acquitted of 'conspiracy to murder' charge.

Sir Anthony Blunt exposed as
Soviet Agent.

PRIVATE SPY

68

v. '79

25p

President Carter foiled in attempts to free American Embassy staff in Teheran.

PRIVATE EYE

79

April '80

30p

HOSTAGES: CARTER'S SHOCK INITIATIVE

Owner of the *Daily Star* Victor Matthews ennobled by Mrs Thatcher.

PRIVATE EYE

483
ay
une '80

30p

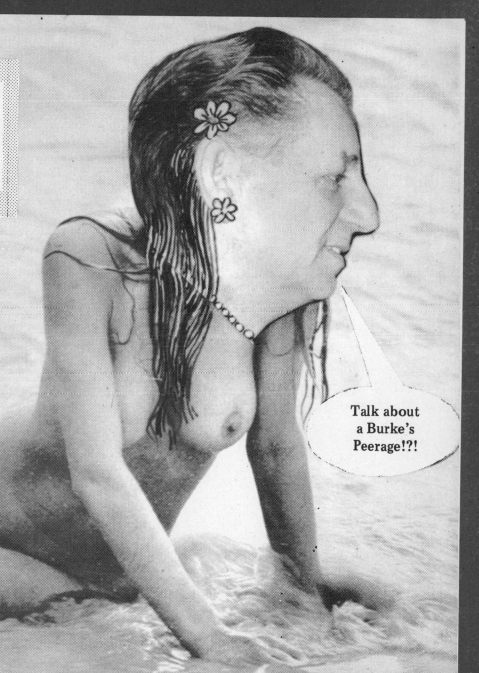

LOVELY "Fingers" Matthews has hit the jackpot.
He's the lucky press-baron who's been given a Life Peerage in the Birthday Honours List.

Picture by RON PORN

Talk about a Burke's Peerage!?!

STARLORD

Unions silent on suppression of Solidarity.

PRIVATE EYE

488

ny

ugust '80

30p

POLAND

MURRAY SPEAKS

Denis Healey fights Michael Foot for Labour Party leadership.

PRIVATE EYE

492
ay
Oct. '80

30p

THEY'RE OFF !

What on earth are you doing, Denis?

I'm keeping a low profile

Leader of the House
Norman St John Stevas
loses his job.

PRIVATE EYE

No. 498
Friday
16 Jan. '81

30p

STEVAS FIRED

Rupert Murdoch buys *'The Times'*.

Rushton drawing shows *Private Eye* characters.

Barbara Cartland is not invited to
the wedding of Prince Charles
and her step-granddaughter
Lady Diana Spencer.

PRIVATE DI

No.512
Friday
1 July '81.

35p

British Rail's new train flops.

Defence Minister John Nott
dispatches a 'Task Force' to
the Falklands.

PRIVATE EYE

530
y
ril '82

35p

Mrs Thatcher is interviewed on
Panorama about her Falklands policy.

PRIVATE EYE

82

35p

INVASION LOOMS

Pope John-Paul II visits Britain.

John Fagan gains access to
Queen's bedroom.

PRIVATE EYE

No. 537
Friday
July '82

35p

ROYAL BREAK·IN SOUVENIR

The Thatchers visit the Falklands.

PRIVATE EYE

550
day,
an. '83

40p

FALKLANDS

That looks like a pub over there!

MAGGIE FLIES IN

Labour leader Michael Foot comes under fire.

PRIVATE EYE

554
ay
arch '83

40p

LABOUR LEADERSHIP
NEW SHOCK

Foreign Secretary Francis Pym
is sacked.

PRIVATE EYE

561
May
June '83

40p

PYM'S GRACEFUL EXIT

Neil Kinnock's car overturns on M4 while he is fighting Roy Hattersley for the Labour leadership.

PRIVATE EYE

564
May
July '83

40p

NEW LABOUR SHOCK

Mrs Thatcher has an eye operation.

PRIVATE EYE
TEST

No. 565
Friday
Aug. '83

40p

Cecil Parkinson 'resigns' as Minister for Trade following 'love child' scandal.

PRIVATE EYE

No. 570
Friday
21 Oct. '83

40p

Wedgwood Benn returns to Parliament as Member for Chesterfield.

PRIVATE EYE

580
ay
arch '84

40p

BENN'S TRIUMPH

I blame the Media